The Old Fashioned Adding-Up Book

The no-nonsense book of practice in basic addition (with answers)

 Ward Lock Educational Co. Ltd.

WARD LOCK EDUCATIONAL CO. LTD.
1 CHRISTOPHER ROAD
EAST GRINSTEAD
SUSSEX RH19 3BT

A MEMBER OF THE LING KEE GROUP
HONG KONG • SINGAPORE • LONDON • NEW YORK

© Marilyn Rivers • Ward Lock Educational Co. Ltd.
All rights reserved. No part of this publication may be reproduced, stored in a retrieval system, or transmitted in any form or by any means, electronic, mechanical, photocopying, recording or otherwise, without the prior written permission of the Publisher.

First published – 1981
Reprinted – 1981,1983,1992

ISBN 0-7062-4086-3

Note to the reader
Pencil in your answers lightly so that you can rub them out and practise again. You can check your answers at the back of the book.

Other titles in this series:
The Old Fashioned Rules of Punctutation Book
ISBN 0 7062 4123 1
The Old Fashioned Rules of Grammar Book
ISBN 0 7062 3850 8
The Old Fashioned Rules of Spelling Book
ISBN 0 7062 4085 5
The Old Fashioned Handwriting Book
ISBN 0 7062 4139 8
The Old Fashioned Multiplication Book
ISBN 0 7062 4121 5
The Old Fashioned Division Book
ISBN 0 7062 4122 3
The Old Fashioned Taking-Away Book
ISBN 0 7062 4148 7
The Old Fashioned Mental Arithmetic Book
ISBN 0 7062 4160 6
The Old Fashioned Times Table Book
ISBN 0 7062 3749 8

Printed in Hong Kong

Add these units.
The first one is done for you.

1. 3 + 4 = 7

2. 2 + 5 =

3. 3 + 6 =

4. 8 + 2 =

5. 9 + 1 =

6. 4 + 4 =

7. 7 + 2 =

8. 5 + 3 =

9. 2 + 4 =

10. 6 + 1 =

11. 1 + 8 =

12. 2 + 6 =

13. 3 + 5 =

14. 7 + 3 =

15. 4 + 5 =

16. 3 + 3 =

17. 6 + 3 =

A unit is a number less than 10.

These units add up to 10.
Fill in the missing unit.

The first one is done for you.

1. 4 + [6] = 10
2. 5 + [ ] = 10
3. 3 + [ ] = 10
4. 1 + [ ] = 10
5. 9 + [ ] = 10
6. 10 + [ ] = 10
7. 2 + [ ] = 10
8. 6 + [ ] = 10
9. 8 + [ ] = 10
10. 7 + [ ] = 10
11. 0 + [ ] = 10

When two units add up to more than 10, you have a ten and a unit, like this:

1. 16 = [1] ten and [6] units.
2. 11 = [1] ten and [ ] units.
3. 13 = [ ] ten and [ ] units.
4. 15 = [ ] ten and [ ] units.
5. 12 = [ ] ten and [ ] units.
6. 19 = [ ] ten and [ ] units.
7. 14 = [ ] ten and [ ] units.
8. 17 = [ ] ten and [ ] units.
9. 18 = [ ] ten and [ ] units.
10. 20 is two tens.
11. 30 is three tens.
12. 40 is [ ] tens.
13. 50 is [ ] tens.
14. [ ] is six tens.
15. 70 is [ ] tens.
16. [ ] is eight tens.
17. 90 is [ ] tens.
18. 100 is ten tens.

Add these units and make a ten and a unit.

1. 9 + 6 = ☐1 ten and ☐5 units = ☐15
2. 3 + 9 = ☐1 ten and ☐ units = ☐
3. 4 + 8 = ☐ ten and ☐ units = ☐
4. 6 + 6 = ☐ ten and ☐ units = ☐
5. 6 + 5 = ☐ ten and ☐ units = ☐
6. 7 + 8 = ☐ ten and ☐ units = ☐
7. 6 + 7 = ☐ ten and ☐ units = ☐
8. 5 + 9 = ☐ ten and ☐ units = ☐
9. 8 + 3 = ☐ ten and ☐ units = ☐
10. 6 + 9 = ☐ ten and ☐ units = ☐
11. 4 + 9 = ☐ ten and ☐ units = ☐
12. 7 + 9 = ☐ ten and ☐ units = ☐
13. 5 + 7 = ☐ ten and ☐ units = ☐
14. 6 + 8 = ☐ ten and ☐ units = ☐
15. 9 + 8 = ☐ ten and ☐ units = ☐
16. 7 + 6 = ☐ ten and ☐ units = ☐
17. 4 + 7 = ☐ ten and ☐ units = ☐

You can also set the sums out this way:

1. 9
   + 6

    15
   ---

2. 3
   + 9
   ---

3. 4
   + 5
   ---

4. 6
   + 6
   ---

5. 7
   + 8
   ---

6. 9
   + 4
   ---

7. 9
   + 8
   ---

8. 10
   + 4
   ---

9. 0
   + 7
   ---

10. 8
   + 9
   ---

11. 6
   + 5
   ---

12. 6
   + 4
   ---

13. 7
   + 9
   ---

14. 8
   + 6

Now you can add tens and units together.

Always add the units column first.
The first one is done for you.

1. T | U

    4 | 2 = [4] tens and [2] units.
    +2 | 1 = [2] tens and [1] unit.

    6 | 3 = [6] tens and [3] units.

2. T | U

    2 | 3 = [ ] tens and [ ] units.
    +3 | 6 = [ ] tens and [ ] units.

    | = [ ] tens and [ ] units.

3. T | U

    1 | 4 = [ ] tens and [ ] units.
    +2 | 5 = [ ] tens and [ ] units.

    | = [ ] tens and [ ] units.

4. T | U

    1 | 2 = [ ] tens and [ ] units.
    +1 | 6 = [ ] tens and [ ] units.

    | = [ ] tens and [ ] units.

5. T | U

    7 | 3 = [ ] tens and [ ] units.
    +1 | 4 = [ ] tens and [ ] units.

    | = [ ] tens and [ ] units.

A practice page of addition sums with tens and units:

Always add the units column first.

1. 42
    + 26

    68
    ----

2. 16
    + 53
    ----

3. 73
    + 25
    ----

4. 34
    + 14
    ----

5. 23
    + 44
    ----

6. 15
    + 24
    ----

7. 31
    + 22
    ----

8. 10
    + 29
    ----

9. 40
    + 40
    ----

10. 16
    + 63
    ----

11. 79
    + 20
    ----

12. 31
    + 16
    ----

13. 43
    + 36
    ----

14. 51
    + 37

When the units column adds up to more than ten, you must carry that ten into the tens column, leaving the units in their answer box.

So, 46 can be done like this:

T	U
4	6
+2	8
①	
7	4

Here are some for you to try.

Always add the units column first.

1.
T	U
2	6
+4	9

2.
T	U
1	5
+3	6

3.
T	U
4	4
+3	7

4.
T	U
2	5
+1	8

5.
T	U
3	9
+5	4

6.
T	U
6	4
+2	8

7.
T	U
6	9
+1	8

8.
T	U
1	8
+5	7

A practice page of more sums.

1.   56
     + 28
        84

2.   44
     + 37
        ___

3.   29
     + 46
        ___

4.   36
     + 58
        ___

5.   17
     + 29
        ___

6.   39
     + 47
        ___

7.   63
     + 19
        ___

8.   72
     + 19
        ___

9.   18
     + 38
        ___

10.   27
      + 24
         ___

11.   49
      + 36
         ___

12.   73
      + 18
         ___

13.   67
      + 23
         ___

14.   42
      + 49
         ___

See if you can use the same method to add hundreds, tens and units. If you make a new hundred move it into the hundreds column.

```
       184        H | T | U
    + 262         1 | 8 | 4
    ─────       + 2 | 6 | 2
                 ①
                 ─────────
                   4 | 4 | 6
```

1. 429   2. 186
  + 236   + 731
  ─────   ─────

3. 508   4. 382
  + 199   + 486
  ─────   ─────

5. 397   6. 489
  + 286   + 347
  ─────   ─────

7. 608   8. 736
  + 149   + 184
  ─────   ─────

9. 552   10. 199
  + 388   + 276
  ─────   ─────

Answers

Page 1
1. — 2. 7 3. 9 4. 10 5. 10 6. 8 7. 9 8. 8 9. 6 10. 7 11. 9 12. 8 13. 8 14. 10 15. 9 16. 6 17. 9

Page 2
1. — 2. 5 3. 7 4. 9 5. 1 6. 0 7. 8 8. 4 9. 2 10. 3 11. 10

Page 3
1. — 2. 1 ten 1 unit 3. 1 ten 3 units 4. 1 ten 5 units 5. 1 ten 2 units 6. 1 ten 9 units 7. 1 ten 4 units 8. 1 ten 7 units 9. 1 ten 8 units 10. — 11. — 12. 4 tens 13. 5 tens 14. 60 15. 7 tens 16. 80 17. 9 tens

Page 4
1. — 2. 1 ten and 2 units = 12 3. 1 ten and 2 units = 12
4. 1 ten and 2 units = 12 5. 1 ten and 1 unit = 11
6. 1 ten and 5 units = 15 7. 1 ten and 3 units = 13
8. 1 ten and 4 units = 14 9. 1 ten and 1 unit = 11
10. 1 ten and 5 units = 15 11. 1 ten and 3 units = 13
12. 1 ten and 6 units = 16 13. 1 ten and 2 units = 12
14. 1 ten and 4 units = 14 15. 1 ten and 7 units = 17
16. 1 ten and 3 units = 13 17. 1 ten and 1 unit = 11

Page 5
1. — 2. 12 3. 9 4. 12 5. 15 6. 13 7. 17 8. 14 9. 7 10. 17
11. 11 12. 10 13. 16 14. 14

Page 6
1. — 2. 59 = 5 tens 9 units 3. 39 = 3 tens 9 units 4. 28 = 2 tens 8 units
5. 87 = 8 tens 7 units

Page 7
1. — 2. 69 3. 98 4. 48 5. 67 6. 39 7. 53 8. 39 9. 80 10. 79
11. 99 12. 47 13. 79 14. 88

Page 8
1. 75 2. 51 3. 81 4. 43 5. 93 6. 92 7. 87 8. 75

Page 9
1. — 2. 81 3. 75 4. 94 5. 46 6. 86 7. 82 8. 91 9. 56 10. 51
11. 85 12. 91 13. 90 14. 91

Page 10
1. 665 2. 917 3. 707 4. 868 5. 683 6. 836 7. 757 8. 920 9. 940
10. 475